Duelling Dories

50 Years of International Dory Racing in Nova Scotia

A.B. Bennet with Garnet Heisler

Research by

Sarah Hubbard, Jill Neidermayer and

Marlene Spindler

Cover and book design: Brenda Conroy
Editing and layout: Richard Rogers
Cover artwork: Ken Lepage

Printed and bound in Canada

Published by Glen Margaret Publishing
P.O. Box 29 Tantallon, Nova Scotia, Canada B0J 3J0
tel./fax: (902-823-1198)
email: richard.rogers@ns.sympatico.ca
www.glenmargaret.com

National Library of Canada Cataloguing in Publication

Bennet, A. B. (Amy Brook), 1964–
    Duelling dories : 50 years of international dory racing
    in Nova Scotia / by A.B. Bennet with Garnet Heisler;
    research by Sarah Hubbard, Jill Neidermayer and
    Marlene Spindler.

ISBN 0-920427-59-6

1. Dories (Boats)—Nova Scotia—History. 2. Rowing—
Nova Scotia—History. I. Heisler, Garnet, 1943- II. Title.

GV832.B45 2002   797.1'4'09716   C2002-902641-5

Dedicated to the memory of
Russell Langille
and
Lloyd Heisler
Dorymates. Champions. Legends.

Acknowledgements

The 2002 Organizing Committe of the Lunenburg Fishermen's Picnic and Reunion is grateful to Marlene Spindler for her extraordinary efforts compiling the Appendix of Champions and Runners-up. Thanks also to Jenny Heisler and Diane Heisler for their help compiling material for the book.

We express, on behalf of spectators, volunteers and rowers past and present, our grateful appreciation to Irving Oil Limited for their generous and on-going support of this event. Irving Oil's dedicated corporate sponsorship has done much to ensure the continued success of the International Dory Races in Nova Scotia.

Contents

To The Citizens of Lunenburg,
As neighbors and friends, we again join with you in this friendly spirit of sportsmanship competition that makes the International Dory Races so interesting and worthwhile.

During times of world tensions and troubles, it is heartening to know that two major nations, yours and mine, can meet in friendly competition, and despite who may win or lose, remain friends and mutual partners in a free world . . .

We wish you the best of luck, friendship and prosperity.

Stanley Eustace, Ipswich, Massachusetts
Member of the Gloucester Committee
From the *Lunenburg Progress Enterprise*
September 20, 1961

Chapter 1

The Workhorse of the North Atlantic

orymates. On the grim seas of the Grand Banks, a small, brightly painted wooden vessel is lowered from the deck of a schooner. Two men, jaws firm, eyes steady, set their oars as the dory touches the water. With their tubs of baited trawl at the ready, they nod to one another and pull. Away from the schooner. Away from their shipmates. Toward the distant horizon. Relying only on each other, and their hardy boat, until the end of the day, when, bone-weary, they will row themselves and their day's catch back across vast grey waters to the relative safety of the schooner.

In communities along the northeast coast of North America this phrase — *dorymates* — is synonymous with partnership. It is a phrase redolent of images, bringing to mind stoic strength, abiding loyalty and the syncopated rhythm of a finely tuned team, hard at work.

"We were dorymates, him and me." In towns and villages where the heritage of the Grand Banks fishery remains, the phrase is still used, even by those who have never been to sea, to convey steadfast companionship. In the same way, it is used to sum up a person's character, for better or worse: *"Let's just say this, you wouldn't want him for a dorymate."* In an age when dories are no longer as commonplace as they once were, the image remains strong in our cultural identity: majestic schooners, golden dories, and tough, stalwart men at the oars.

Although dory-like boats have been in use since about 300 A.D. and can trace their roots back to Egypt and Portugal, it was in the heyday of the Grand Bank fishery that these vessels evolved into the form we are now familiar with. As the "workhorse of the North Atlantic," each aspect of the dory's construction, even the paint job, served a purpose. With a five-to-one length to width ratio, the double-ended little vessels were built to row. The flat bottom and flared side construction ensured a broad, stable vessel that would carry a heavy load, and significantly, the shape allowed dories to be "nested," one inside another, on the deck of a schooner.

The traditional paint job was also designed for the realities of work at sea. The paint of the hull, usually buff or yellow on Nova Scotian dories, allows the boats to be visible against dark waters, and the green trim is easy to pick out against the white backdrop of a thick fog.

In the mid 1800s the concept of trawling for fish using a length of trawl with dozens of baited hooks, instead of hand-lining with a single hook, collided with the evolution of the dory, creating a successful approach to harvesting fish that was to last for nearly a century. From first hand-lining over the side of the schooner, to trawling from the side of the schooner, it became evident that if one could spread fishermen out over the fishing grounds with the means to set and haul trawl themselves, the hold of the schooner could be filled with even greater efficiency. And thus the humble dory entered into the history books. Built to nest and built to row, it was the perfect means to maximize the harvest. In communities like Lunenburg and Shelburne in Nova Scotia along with Glouces-ter, Salisbury and Amesbury in Massachusetts, dory building be-came an industry in itself.

The dory was also indispensable in coastal communities like Mahone Bay, Nova Scotia, where inshore fishing — harvesting fish from waters closer to shore — is still a way of life. In Mahone Bay local lore has it that there is one island for every day of the year. People who populated those islands from the time the area was settled in the mid-1700s relied on the dory as their daily mode of transportation to get to the mainland and to make a living plying the waters. This remained the case until the middle of the twentieth century when motors and motorized boats became ac-cessible and affordable.

Dories used for inshore fishing or life-saving, or even for pleas-ure, will last for decades, but the dories that went to the Banks aboard schooners rarely lasted more than two years. The demands of the task and the stresses of being lowered, hoisted, stacked and lashed to the deck throughout the fishing season took their toll. This was good news for dory-builders. It is estimated that a schooner fleet of 300 would require 2,700 new dories each year.

The men of the Grand Banks depended on their dories for their very lives. Newspaper reports from the late nineteenth and early twentieth centuries recount many tales of dorymen, unable to return to their mother ship in heavy fog or sudden storms, spending days at sea in their small boats. Others took refuge in dories as lifeboats when their ships met with disaster. The April 19, 1911 edition of the *Lunenburg Progress Enterprise* reports on the rescue of Captain Lemuel Ritcey and Captain Zinck of the schooner Hazel L. Ritcey: "*. . . The men were out in their dory fishing when the snow storm came down upon them and shut them off from their vessel. So thick was the weather outside that it was impossible for them to return to their schooner and all day Saturday and Sunday they were at the mercy of the elements in an open dory. When the weather cleared on Monday, the schooner* Tribune *hove in sight and picked up the two exhausted and nearly frozen men . . .*" As memorials in many fishing communities can attest — for every such rescue, there is an equal if not greater number of tragedies. Such was the life, and sometimes death, of a doryman.

In the spirit of the Grand Banks fishery any endeavour could and would be considered a competition. Captains vied for the honour of being declared "High Liner" of the fleet — a designation awarded to the captain who brought in the biggest catch of the season. Fishermen competed to see who could split and salt the most fish when the day's catch was readied for the hold. Whole towns crowed over which community was home port to the faster schooner. And dorymakers established staunch rivalries debating whose boats were the better. (Indeed, suggest to a Lunenburger that a Shelburne dory is a finer boat or visa versa and you'll likely wish that you hadn't.) In the same competitive spirit, dorymen naturally competed, dory against dory, to see which team of rowers was the fastest. It was in those good-natured games that brightened dangerous and demanding days at sea, that traditions and legends were born, and where heroes were made.

Heading out from the schooner for a day's fishing on the Grand Banks.
Courtesy of Knickle's Studio and Gallery, Lunenburg, N.S.

Chapter 2

A Friendly Rivalry Unfolds

S ibling rivalry. It's a description that fits the friendly jousting for bragging rights of all kinds that has taken place for centuries between the fishing villages of Nova Scotia, particularly Shelburne and Lunenburg, and the primary fishing port of New England — Gloucester. Like brothers who test their mettle against one another, yet stand ready to defend the other's honour against outsiders, these fishing communities share a strong bond.

If proof of the connection between Nova Scotia and the town of Gloucester, Massachusetts were needed, it is to be found inscribed on the Gloucester Fishermen's Memorial Cenotaph. There, alongside the names of five thousand, three hundred and sixty eight Gloucestermen are the names of one thousand nine hundred Maritime Canadian fishermen lost at sea from 1846 to the present, while sailing out of Gloucester. There are nineteen Nova Scotians listed for the year 1899 alone.

The June 13, 1888 edition of the Boston Globe describes the relationship between Nova Scotia and Gloucester: "In the spring . . . large numbers of provincials come from Nova Scotia to engage in the mackerel fisheries. They come from the southern portion of that province, and are mainly descendants of loyalists who emigrated from Cape Cod in the revolutionary period. . . . These men are the bravest in the fleet, and no idea can be formed of the risks they take and the dangers they undergo, unless by personal contact and experience with them. They readily assimilate and become citizens."

With their common history and the passionate pride in themselves and their vessels, it was natural for organized competitions to arise between the American and Canadian fishermen. The International Dory Races, an annual event that brings together the best rowers from both sides of the border, could be said to have evolved in some measure from the International Fishermen's Trophy racing series, the series that gave rise to the famed and beloved schooner *Bluenose*. However, it was a shared disdain for cowardice that instigated both the great schooner and dory racing traditions of the New England and Nova Scotia fishing fleets.

In 1920 it blew too hard for the "yachtsmen" who raced in the America's Cup. With twenty three knots of wind predicted, the yacht race was postponed that year. In the opinion of the officials and participants, it would be too dangerous for the sailors and their sailboats to compete in those winds. This, of course, was laughable to Grand Banks fishermen, who regularly sailed in worse conditions. When Senator William Dennis, publisher of the Halifax Herald, heard the news of the America's Cup postponement, he was inspired to come up with a challenge that would show the dandies of the New York Yacht Club what real sailors were made of. Dennis launched the "Halifax Herald North Atlantic Fishermen's International Competition," the first formalized event to celebrate the skills and pride of the fishing fleets and to recognize the tradition of friendly rivalry that existed between the "Novies" and the "Yanks." To ensure that his trophy challenge would always retain the true essence of the schooner fleets, Dennis ruled that all competing vessels must have worked at least one season in the fishery.

In the fall of 1920, the Lunenburg schooner *Delawana* and the Gloucester schooner *Elsie* met to compete for the first Fishermen's Trophy challenge, each vessel having won the right to represent its country by way of local elimination heats. Nova Scotian pride was badly bruised when *Elsie* defeated *Delawana* two races to one in the three race series, sailing back to Gloucester with the trophy and $4,000 in prize money.

This was not what Senator Dennis had expected. Determined to prove Nova Scotia's superiority on the seas, he gathered a group of wealthy investors and commissioned William J. Roue to design and build a schooner that would win back the trophy. Then he sought out the man who would captain the vessel: Captain Angus Walters from Lunenburg. In March of 1921, Roue's masterpiece, the schooner *Bluenose* was launched from the Smith and Rhuland Shipyard in Lunenburg, and Angus Walters took the helm as she headed to the fishing grounds.

They met the American vessel *Elsie* in heavy winds in the fall of '21, thrilling the nation as the Canadians won handily with a three mile lead. In the racing series that continued to be held sporadically until 1938, Captain Walters and the *Bluenose* were never defeated. She remains the greatest schooner of all time. A fine fishing vessel and the defender of Bluenose pride.

In the seasons when she was working, boys from Lunenburg County vied for a chance to fish aboard the revered *Bluenose*, and to learn from her respected captain. Among those lads who spent a season or two learning the ropes aboard the legendary vessel was a boy from Rous Island in Mahone Bay named Lloyd Heisler. Perhaps it was in the foc'sle of the *Bluenose* that Lloyd, who was to become a folk hero of Nova Scotia, would hear first hand the tales of victory over Gloucestermen. This would foreshadow the undefeated greatness he, like the *Bluenose,* would achieve.

During the years when the *Bluenose* was gracefully denying victory to her Gloucester competitors, the tradition of an end-of-summer celebration for the fleets originated. In Lunenburg, fishermen would gather for what would become the Nova Scotia Fisheries Exhibition & Fishermen's Picnic, held then in September. It was a chance for the fishermen to enjoy a summer celebration with their families and compete against each other using the skills of their trade. The main event of these gatherings was the dory races, with teams pulling their oars over a mile long set course in Lunenburg Harbour. In Gloucester, at their annual St. Peter's Fiesta in June, similar events took place with the strongest, most able rowers competing for glory in their homeport.

In Lunenburg, Lloyd Heisler from Rous Island off Indian Point and his friend Russell Langille, from Oakland had dominated the local dory racing competitions for years. With the gregarious Heisler, a massive man built of hard muscle, in the bow and the quiet Langille, tall and lean, in the stern, the two had perfected their style over years of rowing together. Heisler and Langille con-

Dories on the line in Lunenburg Harbour
Courtesy of Knickle's Studio and Gallery, Lunenburg, N.S.

sidered themselves just "a couple of hayseeds who row now and again." They established a habit of getting together for a good luck drink before their races and always had a drink to celebrate after. They even claimed to carry a bottle with them in the dory, so they could stop for a small nip if the race was an easy one and they were ahead by a wide enough margin. But once the gun went off, they were nothing but grace. Fluid and smooth as dancers, they pulled with such power that spectators sometimes accused them jokingly of having "a motor on board."

What was it that made Lloyd Heisler the champion dory racer that he was? His wife Jenny, now in her late nineties, admits with a small smile and a gleam in her bright eyes that "Lloyd wasn't much of one to practise. It was just something he was good at." But Charles Bonnell, a neighbour who grew up on nearby Zwicker's Island and a lifelong friend of Lloyd and Jenny's son Garnet, attributes the rowing success that would find the Heisler family for decades to something else: "It was a hard life on the islands. We had no electricity until 1961. Just about every part of your life involved hard work. If you needed to go to the mainland, you rowed. You needed to go fishing or hunting to feed your family, you rowed. You wanted to go to school in the winter, you

14

had to get the snow out of your punt, free the line tying it from the ice, drag it to the water and row to school. That's the way it was. . . the Heislers worked a small farm and Lloyd did some fishing. There was nothing soft in that life. You got by with hard work and nothing else — it made for tough men who were good with a pair of oars."

Whether he needed to or not, Russell Langille did practise. He would row alone — Lloyd didn't make time for formal practises — setting a stopwatch on the wharf and rowing out to the nearest island, pulling hard to get to the island and back in ten minutes.

The style of the two men differed in many ways. Lloyd, with his huge hands and powerful build, was a colourful story teller with a crushing handshake. He was undeniably a force to be reckoned with physically and possessed a character that commanded attention. Russell, on the other hand, was a gentle soul who said little - content for the most part to let Lloyd lead the way. When a competitor remarked to Lloyd before a race on one occasion that Russell didn't seem to have much to say, Lloyd informed the man that it didn't matter, Russell could "row like hell and has eyes in the back of his head."

Year after year, Lloyd and Russell took on all challengers at the dory races held at the annual Exhibition in Lunenburg and defeated every team they faced. Then in the winter of 1951, Lloyd met up with a fellow fisherman from Gloucester, Tom Frontiero, over drinks in a Lunenburg bar. Bragging was the order of the evening and the talk soon turned to dory races. Both men claimed the superiority of their local rowers. There was only one way to settle the issue. Frontiero went back to Gloucester with the germ of an idea planted in his mind.

The call came in to Captain Rollie Knickle and Lunenburg businessman Ray Tanner in June of 1952. Tanner and Knickle were both heavily involved in organizing the watersports events of the Lunenburg exhibition. A challenge had been issued from Gloucester: bring your best men and we'll race you — see which town really produces the finer dory rowers. There was no doubt in the minds of Tanner and Knickle as to who should row for Lunenburg. Heisler and Langille were the men for the job.

"Maybe they were sick of the *Bluenose* beating their boats all those years," Garnet Heisler says with a laugh when he talks about the racing series that would lead his father Lloyd to the Nova Scotia Sports Hall of Fame. "Maybe they really thought this was something they could finally beat us at!"

Whatever the motivation — Heisler's unshakeable bravado in a waterfront bar, or the dream of defeating Lunenburg on the water after years of looking at the stern end of the *Bluenose* — Gloucester had issued the challenge. The gauntlet had been thrown down.

Chapter 3

The 1950s – Heisler and Langille – All the Way

In fifteen consecutive years of racing at the Fisheries Exhibition, Heisler and Langille had never been beaten. It was that track record that had Ray Tanner knocking on their doors looking for someone to go to Gloucester to race against the Americans. Heisler and Langille were up for the challenge. "If I remember correctly," Ray Tanner told Chronicle Herald and Mail Star newspaper reporter Linda Mason in 1982, "their answer was they would go if I brought the liquid refreshments and I agreed."

With Captain Rollie Knickle, the two rowers jumped in Tanner's car and headed for Massachusetts. No real discussion about the structure of the race had taken place before the Lunenburg contingent arrived in Gloucester. It came as a surprise then to Heisler and Langille, that the Gloucestermen, who usually rowed seine boats, raced with four oarsmen and a steerer to a dory, and it was an equal shock to the Gloucester organizers that the Lunenburgers raced with only two. Lloyd, in his inimitable way, lightened the awkward situation. "It's alright," he told them. "You race with four against the two of us. We'll beat you anyway." The Gloucestermen could see, that in spite of his grin, Heisler wasn't kidding.

In the end, two of Gloucester's best men, Jerry Nicastro and Ion Stephe (Steve) d'Amico were selected to compete against the Heisler- Langille duo. Captain Rollie Knickle had observed the Gloucester team practising and had reported to Heisler and Langille that it looked like they would be hard to beat. Nicastro was 27 and d'Amico was 25. Heisler and Langille were 45 and 48 respectively.

But as it turned out, there was no advantage in youth that day on the Gloucester waterfront.

Using the years of experience to their credit and a lifetime of hard-earned muscle power, combined with the magic of their well-honed stroking technique, the Lunenburg team took the early lead and kept it. After rounding the buoy neatly, Heisler and Langille took note of their significant lead and, according to those who watched, seemed to hold back not wanting to humiliate their hosts with a devastating defeat. Serafino (Sophie) Frontiero, one of the original four Gloucestermen selected to race who had given up his place in the dory when the team was reduced to two, describes the scene: "On the way home they (*Heisler and Langille*) opened up a comfortable margin and then showed their class and sportsmanship by easing up and not making a rout of the race, which they could have easily done. I knew that the crowd and I had just watched greatness."

Heisler's account of the race was succinct: "We took the lead and walked right home with the trophy. To top it all off, those fellows were half our age."

After the post-race parties and the presentation of the trophy,

The first international dory racing champions, Lloyd Heisler(left) and Russell Langille.
Courtesy of Geno Mondello, Gloucester, Mass.

it was agreed that Gloucester would send a team to compete against Canada at the Fisheries Exhibition in Lunenburg in the fall. And with that the International Dory Racing tradition was firmly established — a tradition that has carried on from those innocent days of the 1950s, when families like the Heislers lived without electricity, to these days of the new millennium and a fast-paced wired world.

That first year and in the five decades that have followed, the dory races in Gloucester were marked with a gracious hospitality and camaraderie that would become legendary among Lunenburg rowers and their families. It was the perk that came with winning the right to compete for Canada. The competition on the water was undoubtedly intense, but you were guaranteed that the people of Gloucester would welcome you with warmth and treat you like lifelong friends. Ray Tanner remarked many years later that the dory races had made Gloucester his second home. At that first race, Lloyd Heisler and Russell Langille were the guests of Gloucester Mayor Joe Grillo who treated the men to world-class hospitality. Sherman Zwicker, who would become Mayor of Lunenburg, and who took on the role of organizing the Lunenburg exhibition watersports after Ray Tanner stepped down, recalls that he had his first taste of pizza courtesy of the Gloucester dory racing crowd during his first visit to Massachusetts in 1955. "They certainly showed us a fine time, going all out to plan events and parties for the Lunenburgers. Our colleagues in Gloucester would even take visiting Lunenburgers into Boston to tour the city. They have always been exceptional hosts and good friends."

Basking in the glow of their win and the good fun of their visit to Gloucester, Knickle, Tanner, Heisler and Langille returned to Lunenburg to ready their home port for the arrival of the Americans in the fall and to defend supremacy of the Canadian rowing tradition.

It was September 16th, 1952 when a large crowd gathered on the Lunenburg waterfront to watch the duelling dories at the first international competition in Lunenburg Harbour. The Gloucester contingent had arrived in style aboard a U.S. Coast Guard cutter with a delegation of supporters to cheer on their team. On the day of the race, Gloucester sent rowers Fred Purdy and Winthrop

Davis to the line to pull for American glory. For Lunenburg and Canada, it was naturally Heisler and Langille on the line again.

From the sound of the starting gun, oars dug deep into the harbour waters, the two boats gliding bow to bow for the first fifty yards. With Heisler nursing a sprained back and an American team that had trained well over the summer, learning from the June defeat of their countrymen, this race was not going to be the walk in the park that Heisler and Langille had experienced a few months earlier in Gloucester waters.

The rowers battled each other with Lunenburg taking no more than a lead of two dory lengths before the turning buoy. Once again, though, experience came through. With Russell Langille's innate ability to guide a dory straight and true, and Lloyd Heisler's machinelike power, the Canadians nursed a fifteen second lead heading into the home stretch and victory, crossing the finish line marked by the Fisheries Patrol vessel *Lacuna* with thirty-four seconds to spare. Accepting the trophy presented by Gloucester Mayor Joe Grillo, Lloyd Heisler and Russell Langille marked their eighteenth win together, and their first international win in Canada, to the cheers of an adoring hometown crowd.

The history of the dory races is full of rich anecdotes, many enhanced by time and the retelling of those who where there. One such tale has been told time and time again. With Ray Tanner once again driving Heisler and Langille to Gloucester, the group was zipping through Annapolis Royal, heading for Digby where they would board a Canadian naval vessel for the rest of the journey. Ray Tanner was leaning a little heavily on the accelerator, as he was known to do, when the lights of a police car appeared in the rearview mirror and the sound of a siren filled the car.

Ray Tanner described the incident to a newspaper reporter: "After a lengthy explanation as to where we were going and who the two were in the back seat, the constable let us go — with a warning that if Russell and Lloyd did not win for Canada, then he would make them pay a fine when they returned." No fine was necessary as the invincible pair won again.

After returning to Gloucester in the summer of 1953, and taking the trophy for a third time (retiring that particular trophy on the merit of their triple win as it would now be theirs to keep) the pair announced in a post-race interview that they would not race again. They were both now approaching fifty and had rowed together and competed for close to twenty years. It seemed like time to step aside.

During their years of competition, the Heisler-Langille duo had developed great respect for two fishermen from Herring Cove, a village outside of Halifax, Nova Scotia. Heisler described the Herring Cove team of Dick Nagle and Gerald Dempsey as " a tough pair to beat." And it was Dempsey and Nagle who would win the Canadian elimination races in Lunenburg, earning them the right to represent Canada in the International competition in Lunenburg after Heisler and Langille put away their oars.

Mary Dauphinee, a spectator at the Lunenburg Exhibition where Dempsey and Nagle squared off against the Americans, re-corded the action for the provincial newspaper, writing:

"The instant the signal sounded the dories surged forward as though propelled by some power greater than human muscles and human will. Men, dories and oars moved in beautiful unison. Quickly the Canadian team pulled slightly ahead of the Gloucester boys. . . There was no clapping of the hands yet. Just quiet appraisal of the strength, skill and endurance of the youthful oarsmen as they pulled madly toward the black buoys a half a mile away."

It was a thrilling finish that day as both teams fought with everything they possessed to win. If the energy of the crowd gives anything to an athlete, there was a lift there on that September day for Nagle and Dempsey as the crowd screamed and roared for another Canadian victory. Pouring on their last ounce of might the team from Herring Cove pulled ahead by a mere three feet just as they approached the finish, giving their countrymen the win they so badly wanted.

The Herring Cove fishermen would have their chance to ex-perience the famed St. Peter's Fiesta in Gloucester, to enjoy the parties and hospitality of their American hosts, and to defend their champion status in June of 1954. Having competed unsuccessfully against Heisler and Langille so many times and being denied the opportunity to go on to international competition, the pair made the most of their chance at glory in the U.S. waters and proudly took home top honours. But it was to be their only shot at a trip

Trophy Day in Lunenburg 1953. From left, Janet Conrad, Fred Purdy, Edward Josephson, Dick Nagle, Gerald Dempsey, and Claire Bailly.

Courtesy of the Creaser family

to Gloucester, for at the Canadian elimination races in September Heisler and Langille were back. Retirement wasn't for them. The urge to compete was too strong. They wanted another shot at the title. And they would go on to win it three more times: in Lunenburg in 1954, and Gloucester and Lunenburg in 1955.

Sherman Zwicker, having accepted the chairmanship of the watersports event in Lunenburg, recalls the roguish charm that made Lloyd such a popular figure. "It was the trip to Gloucester in June of 1955. After the race, which Lloyd and Russell won, there was a huge crowd gathered around them on the wharf. Lloyd struck quite a figure, in the white undershirt and dark trousers he wore to race. I suppose you could say the women were drawn to his magnetism. That day on the wharf one woman asked him in an awestruck voice, 'Mr. Heisler, how did you get such big muscles?' 'My dear lady,' Lloyd boomed, grinning, 'I'm a farmer. I've got four cows at home that need milking morning and night. So I pull sixteen teats twice a day. I believe that's where these here muscles come from.' Well, I can tell you," recalls Zwicker, " that woman blushed beet red and Lloyd just went on grinning."

By now, Lloyd and Russell were truly established folk heroes. Their undefeated, heroic efforts at the oars, the charm of Russell's gentlemanly nature and Lloyd's exuberance, along with their willingness to share advice and ideas with up and coming rowers made them popular with the crowds and their competitors alike.

After winning the trophy in Gloucester that June of 1955, the revered pair would return to Lunenburg and the Canadian elimination races, where they would have what was perhaps the toughest race of their careers, rowing against seven other teams. On the day of the elimination races, it came down to what was essentially a race between three pairs. Heisler and Langille fought hard with a dory rowed by Gerald Hannams and Gerald Schwartz close on them all the way. Hard behind Hannams and Schwartz was Herring Cove's Dick Nagle, who was rowing that year with a new partner, a strapping young man of seventeen named Sonny Heisler. Lloyd's older boy.

After winning the eliminations, Lloyd and Russell once again faced down their American counterparts in front of a crowd of thousands on the Lunenburg waterfront. In their preferred style, the Canadians took an early lead and nursed it all the way, finishing six dory lengths in front of Gloucester's Warren MacGregor and James Carter. As they raised their oars in victory, a wave of sustained applause from the throng swept over Lloyd and Russell. After proving themselves this one last time in front of their home town crowd, they were finished. They would not race again.

The torch was thrown that September day to Gerald Schwartz and his partner Gerald Hannams. With Heisler and Langille retired, Schwartz and Hannams, with their second place finish in the Canadian elimination races, had earned the right to travel to Gloucester to row for Canada. For Schwartz it was a well-deserved honour that had been a long time coming. He had rowed in the Lunenburg races since 1932, having the ill-fortune of going up against Heisler and Langille year after year.

Schwartz and Hannams would do Canada proud, there was no doubt. It was right and proper that they should take up the mantle placed upon them by the retiring champions. But watch-

Heroes Heisler (far right) and Langille (third from left) share the media limelight with their American counterparts, Bunt Davis (second from right) and William Merchant (second from left). Gerald Regan, who would go on to be premier of Nova Scotia, is pictured on the far left.

Courtesy of Geno Mondello

ing on the wharf that day, seeing their father take the trophy for his last time, seeing Schwartz and Hannams accept responsibility for defending Canada's pride were Sonny Heisler and his younger brother Garnet. Both were confident that their time would come.

Chapter 4

A New Era Begins

W hat's the matter? Your arms broke?" Garnet Heisler can hear the words ringing in his ears just as clearly today as he heard them back when he was a small boy rowing his punt to school on the mainland from his home on Rous Island. Watching his brother, Sonny, six years Garnet's senior, putt past in his motorized skiff, Garnet would sometimes ask for a tow the mile or so to shore.

"I should have learned, I suppose," says Garnet, "His answer was always the same. He'd ask me if my arms were broke, then he'd smirk and motor past. You can imagine, it got under my skin." Sonny's was a prophetic question though, as broken bones and rowing would later come to enhance the Heisler legend in dory racing circles.

In the spartan life of their childhood on Rous Island with their mother Jenny and their father Lloyd, the Heisler boys worked for everything and there were no excuses. Sonny had earned the money to purchase his boat and motor by lobstering and fishing. Garnet was still too young to have earned such luxuries and, until then, he would row with nothing short of broken limbs as excuse enough to slack off.

From their earliest memories, life was about work for the Heisler boys. Living a self-sufficient life on their farm with no electricity, everyone in the family contributed: from making hay together in the summers, to fixing fence, to fishing and lobstering. "When I was fifteen," says Garnet, "my job was to milk four cows in the morning and haul six of our sixty five lobster traps and then row over to Indian Point for twenty after eight in the morning to pick up the school bus to go to Mahone Bay school. Every morning. And let me tell you, hauling and setting lobster traps from a dory is just damn hard work."

Both Lloyd and Jenny instilled in their boys a staunch work ethic by setting a remarkable example for them. Jenny not only handled the household chores, but also worked alongside her husband and sons in the hayfield and gardens, and held the fort when Lloyd was away fishing or competing. Lloyd, with no formal schooling, taught his boys the meaning of self-reliance. "Those fellows inshore fishing, setting hundreds of traps and hand-lining," says Garnet. "Those were iron men. They don't make them like that any more, because if they did, you would recognize them."

When it came to rowing, both Garnet and Sonny simply figured that if their dad could do it, so could they. They had seen the pleasure and renown their father had gained from his dory racing experiences. They grew up listening to Lloyd's tales of travelling to the United States and the good times and great friends he and Russell had found in international competition. It was a natural evolution then, that like their father before them, Sonny and Garnet would want to row their way to glory.

In the wake of Lloyd and Russell's retirement in 1955, Schwartz and Hannams, then Dempsey and Nagle, would ably hold on to the titles in Gloucester and Lunenburg through 1956 and 1957, continuing to deny the United States a win on the water. It was, by now, generally acknowledged that the dory races had taken up where the International Fishermen's Trophy schooner races had left off, and the United States had yet to taste victory.

That would change in June of 1959 when Charles Moon and Robert Harrington — a pair of twenty three year old clam diggers from Ipswich, Massachusetts, just twelve miles down the coast from Gloucester — would meet Dempsey and Nagle at the line. The Americans pulled ahead at the turning buoy and fought off the Canadians to hold their lead down to the finish, winning the trophy for the United States for the first time by a mere nine seconds.

June of 1959 was ripe with success for the Gloucester rowers. A new division had been introduced to the international competitions. Junior and female rowers had been competing in both Lunenburg and Gloucester local events at the Exhibition and St.

Canadians David Creaser (left) and Cyril Ernst congratulate their American counterparts.

Courtesy of the Creaser family.

Peter's Fiesta respectively, but in 1959 the decision was made to open up junior competition to the international level. In the first junior race, cousins Leonard and Gordon Eisnor from Indian Point, Mahone Bay took up the oars for Canada, while Carlton Eckborg and George Hastings represented the United States. Eckborg and Hastings, a team that weighed in at one hundred and fifty pounds heavier even than the senior Gloucester team, took that first international junior challenge. This gave the Americans a sweet double victory, the Gloucester papers noting, "The Nova Scotians warmly congratulating the winning Americans."

For the remainder of the 1950s, the trophies would be hotly contested with victories going back and forth between Canada and the U.S in the senior division, and the Eisnor cousins picking up four trophies in the junior ranks. The dawn of the new decade of the 1960s brought a thrilling race in Gloucester when Canadian champions David Creaser and Cyril Ernst won in a time of six minutes and eight seconds, the fastest on record. "We have rowed harder races," David Creaser told reporters, "but none faster." And the 1960s would bring the Heisler name back to the dory racing headlines of the day.

Sonny Heisler had been competing for a few years with different partners in the dory, but in 1960 for the Canadian eliminations, Sonny had hooked up with his friend Leonard Eisnor, the former junior champion now rowing in the senior division. It was a combination that worked. Sonny and Leonard won the right to represent Canada against the Gloucestermen at the Lunenburg Exhibition.

In the juniors, young Garnet Heisler paired up with his cousin Lawrence (Lolly) Ernst who had also been born on Rous Island. Coached by Russell Langille, the team won the right to represent Canada in the junior competition.

On the day of the 1960 international competition in Lunenburg, Sonny and Leonard blew the competition away, winning with ease. Meanwhile, Garnet and Lolly were in a dogfight for the junior title, but pulled a win out of the close battle. The headlines in the local paper read: Indian Point Oarsmen Win Both International Dory Races. For the next five international competitions, those same four Indian Point oarsmen, Sonny and Leonard, Garnet and Lawrence would win both senior and junior divisions in Gloucester and Lunenburg.

In the fall of 1963 Leonard Eisnor was recovering from an operation, and Lolly Ernst had to go to Halifax for a vocational exam. Garnet Heisler was no longer eligible to race in the junior division, and both brothers were left without a partner. Sonny asked Garnet if he would row with him in the Canadian eliminations to try to qualify to race against the Americans.

"You have to understand," Garnet says looking back, "me and Sonny had never gotten along with each other. Just an older brother/younger brother thing — probably just that he was six years older and didn't want a young pup like me hanging around with him and his friends. But in all those years on the island, working together side by side in the hayfield, sitting beside each other at the dinner table, we never had much to say to one another. Never had that much to do with one another really. So when Sonny asked me if I wanted to row with him, well, that was something else."

And row together they did. Garnet describes their first efforts.

The Heisler brothers Sonny (right) and Garnet taking the turn in Gloucester.

Used with the permission of the Gloucester Daily Times, *Gloucester Mass.*

"Through my junior years and all Sonny's years of rowing, we'd both been in the bow. So that was a bit of a challenge. Who was going to row bow? So what we did was, we went out two nights in a row — the first night him in the bow, the second night me in the bow and we took our times. We were faster with me in the bow, and that's the way it would stay. I was known for keeping a dory on a true course and that's the job of the fella in the bow. And the guy in the stern, well, he needs to put his head down and pull. And by God, Sonny was good at that."

The day of the Canadian elimination races, the Heisler boys rowed together with matchless grace as if indeed it was something they had been born to do. For those who watched that first race that the Heisler brothers rowed together, it brought back images of an earlier era.

"To see Dad and Russell in a dory — they were a machine, they were just a machine. And people said the same when they saw Sonny and I in a dory. The dory just seemed like it was laughing. It was just laughing."

When they shipped their oars after crossing the finish line, winning their first race together, Sonny Heisler turned to his younger brother, holding his hand out to him. "Good job, brother," he said.

"That was the first time in my life that I shook my brother's hand," recalls Garnet, "and it changed everything. That was the beginning of us getting along together." Lloyd was there watching his boys win together that day, "and don't you think he wasn't a happy lad" Garnet remembers.

With both Sonny and Garnet rowing in the senior division, the United States oarsmen came into their own in the juniors. From September 1963 when Ronald Ottens and Richard Greeke from Massachusetts thrilled the crowd with their homeport junior victory, until September of 1967, the Americans won every junior division title in both Gloucester and Lunenburg. In those years, one name from Gloucester would be recorded again and again: that name was Hilary Dombrowski. Rowing with partners Philip Hoystradt and later Ronald Woodard, Dombrowski captured the junior trophy four times.

The Americans were serious about their training and practising. High school students in New England could participate in dory racing through school programs, and former American champions like Warren MacGregor, who had duelled with Heisler and Langille, were committed to coaching the young rowers.

At home in Canada, Sonny and Garnet took a different approach, relying on their natural talent and less on practise. And it would come to haunt them.

In 1964 at Gloucester, Sonny tied a green garbage bag around the cast that ran from his toes to his knee to protect it from getting wet, then gently lowered himself into the dory where his brother waited. The two had a quick chat about strategy, deciding that they needed a good jump at the start so that Sonny would have time to move his broken foot up to the gunnels, where he could reposition for the long strokes needed later in the race. That decided, they headed to the start, calm and confident — after all, it wasn't as if Sonny's arms were broken.

The Heislers got their quick start. Sonny got his foot up, and they rowed home with a comfortable lead of a dory length and a half. The boys were starting to get cocky.

After winning again in Lunenburg that fall, Sonny and Garnet returned to Gloucester in June of 1965 to row against the successful pair of Robert Greeke and Philip Hoysradt. The American pair had been touted as the strongest Gloucester team to challenge the Heisler brothers yet, but once again Sonny and Garnet grabbed the win by using a technique similar to that of their father and Russell Langille. "We liked to get a good start then, after we have opened things up, we change our stroke from a short hard stroke to a long, gliding stroke." Sonny would change the tempo, calling out to Garnet, "Catch up to this one." That was the key phrase for the shift in the rhythm, their favoured weapon.

In the fall, the brothers took on Hoysradt and Greeke again in Lunenburg and once again came out victorious. Then the Heisler boys shipped their oars and spent the winter focussing on their jobs and on their families.

Sonny and Garnet arrived in Gloucester in June of 1966, out of shape by their own accounts. Their decisive wins in the previous season over a team thought to be contenders made them lax over the long winter months.

"Dad was telling us there was no need to practise, and we were both so busy with work," says Garnet, "we didn't really worry about it. We thought we could just go down and do what we always did — win."

They hadn't counted on Hilary Dombrowski and his new partner John (Jack) Sulton. Dombrowski and Sulton, both still teenagers, had spent the months since April putting in endless hours of practise. They were fit and working like a well-oiled machine by the time June rolled around. Hilary was an experienced junior champion, but he wanted more. What he and Jack Sulton wanted more than anything was to beat the famous Heisler brothers in front of a Gloucester crowd.

Sonny recalls, "I was confident before we went over to Gloucester, but when I heard how hard they had been practising, I knew it was going to be a tough one. It was too."

Neck and neck from the gun, the Heislers never had a chance to lengthen their stroke. The strong young American boys were pulling as if each stroke would be their last, staying right with the Canadian boat, Jack's oars and Sonny's splashing almost together. The Heislers were pouring their entire beings into their oars fighting for every inch. "We might have been ahead for a second near the turn," Sonny remembers, "but that was it. It was that close."

Garnet describes the finish. "The crowds were running along the wharf — this was in Gloucester, you understand — these were their boys. Hilary and Jack had a chance to defeat us Canadians, and Heislers at that. The crowd was giving them quite a lift. And they took us by six feet."

At the finish, Garnet, completely depleted, collapsed in exhaustion and was taken by ambulance to hospital. Later that evening, after he and Sonny had spoken, Garnet announced that he'd had enough of dory racing. He wanted to concentrate on his work and his home life. Even when they won, the $200 prize money that he split with Sonny didn't cover the cost of time lost from work to row. Sonny was determined to carry on, and vowed to find a new partner to help him regain the title in Lunenburg and re-establish a legacy of winning.

The next decade and a half of senior's dory racing in Canada and the United States was all about Sonny Heisler. Learning from his defeat at the oars of fitter, more-practised young Americans, Sonny was determined not to make the same lackadaisical mistake again.

Chapter 5

Years of Change

It was red-headed Gerald Mossman, a wiry, energetic young man, that Sonny Heisler selected to take Garnet's place in the bow of his dory. "I guess it was a good balance," Mossman says of his partnership with Sonny Heisler, referring to both their physical beings and their attitudes. "When we started together I weighed 180 pounds and Sonny weighed 185, so that kept the boat in good trim. And I guess I was kind of the hyper one. Always worried that the competition was gaining on us. Sonny stayed calm. Almost laid back, but boy, he was there when we needed it. So with me being so wound up, and Sonny so cool, I guess we made a pretty good team."

Together Sonny and Gerald would take twelve international trophies over the next six years. That first September of 1966, with Gerald in the bow for the first time, Heisler and Mossman faced the team that had defeated Sonny and Garnet in Gloucester — Dombrowski and Sulton. Mossman had been going to school in Sydney, Nova Scotia (a six hour drive from Lunenburg). With Gerald at school in Sydney, the Canadians didn't have much opportunity to practise together. Sonny, though, had rowed himself into shape and worked hard to be fit for another show down with the young oarsmen from Gloucester.

It was an exciting duel. For once, a Heisler was the underdog. Sonny had something to win back and somebody he needed to beat. In spite of the lack of practise with his partner Gerald, the Canadians came together and built up a good lead by the time they got to the turning buoy. "They were coming on strong at the end," Gerald remembers. "And it was a close race, but we beat them. It was pretty satisfying."

Sonny Heisler (left) and Gerald Mossman (right) with champions of an earlier era, Lloyd Heisler (second from left) and Dick Nagle.
Courtesy of Knickle's Studio and Gallery, Lunenburg, N.S.

With the strong finish put on by Dombrowski and Sulton, the next showdown in Gloucester (where the course is longer) was built up by fans and the press as the race where the American team would once again win the trophy in their home port.

But it wasn't meant to be. Mossman and Heisler, both now living in Lunenburg County, were practising together regularly. They had found their rhythm and were ready in June of 1967 when they went to Gloucester. "We beat them hands down," Mossman remembers. The team of Heisler and Mossman never looked back — and they were never beaten in the next ten international competitions nor in the Canadian elimination races they entered.

In their years together, Sonny and Gerald witnessed some exciting times and had some interesting adventures.

In 1970 a delegation of about thirty-five oarsmen, supporters and committee members travelled to Gloucester for the races —

Heisler and Mossman (left) battling rivals Hilary Dumbrowski and Jack Sulton (in sunglasses) in Gloucester, 1967.

Courtesy of Gerald & Maureen Mossman

one of the best representations in years. As was the custom, a Canadian Coast Guard Ship carried the Lunenburg contingent to and from Gloucester. The vessel enlisted for the job in 1970 was CCGS *Alert*. The *Alert* departed the New England port early in the morning, but at four o'clock a fire broke out in the engine room. Unable to extinguish the blaze at first, the crew and passengers were mustered to the boat stations and a call for help was sent out over the radio. Several vessels in the area responded quickly, but, in the meantime, the crew members battling the fire were able to get it under control and finally extinguish it. The *Alert* with her complement of dory racers and fans was then able to head home to Lunenburg under reduced speed. The stories of the Canadian wins in both the seniors and juniors were somewhat eclipsed in the aftermath by stories of the shipboard fire!

The Lunenburg dory races held that September also stand out in the minds of those who took part, but for different reasons. It was scandal, not potential disaster that marked the Lunenburg event

35

in 1970.

No one has ever confessed to the tampering that resulted in the cancellation of the official junior races that year, but whoever sabotaged the dories certainly knew what they were doing. On the evening before the Canadian junior races, when everyone had finished their final practice row for the day and the dories were bobbing at their mooring ropes, someone painstakingly attached a bucket to the bottom of each boat. Using a length of rope and marine screws, the buckets were made fast in such a way as to be both secure and unnoticeable.

When the dories were lined up at the start the next morning, the oarsmen could sense something was wrong from before the time the gun went off. Garnet Heisler was then coaching the junior champions Reid Risser and David Croft. "The boys had had trouble getting to the line. They thought there was something wrong with them — it was so hard to row. They couldn't imagine why their rowing was so sluggish." The jostling for position at the start line paid off for Reid and David though. The line attaching the bucket to the bottom of their dory caught on the buoy chain at the start. When they pulled for the jump off the line, they wrenched the bucket off the end of the rope securing it to the bottom of their dory.

"David and Reid won the thing by a mile, of course," Garnet remembers, "Everyone else was pulling like mad men trying to get something going, not knowing what the hell was happening. For a while after the race, people thought it was Reid and David who had done the tampering because they won, and by a huge margin, but when the boats were pulled out, with the line and the screws there on their boat, you could see that theirs had been sabotaged just like everyone else's. They'd just managed to lose the bucket by chance."

Uproar ensued. Some people wanted to blame the American contingent, but there was no proof that it was an American or Americans who had meddled with the dories. Others were simply outraged and wanted to cancel the entire international dory racing event, considering it tainted by such unsportsmanlike conduct.

Sherman Zwicker, then a member of the Exhibition commit-

Gerald Mossman (third from right) and Sonny Heisler
(second from right) accept congratulations from Prime
Minister Pierre Elliot Trudeau, while junior champions
George Taylor (far left) and Tim Atkinson (second from left)
look on.

Courtesy of Gerald & Maureen Mossman

tee remembers, "It was really the only time there were any bad feelings at all connected with the dory races. Sure, the juniors were sometimes a little more intense with their competitors off the water, that's just the posturing of youth. The seniors and committee members from both countries were almost all good friends who could leave the spirit of competition at the finish line. So this was something completely different. People were very upset at the thought of someone trying to cheat".

In the end, the senior competitions went forward as scheduled, but the record books show that there was no official race for the juniors that year; although Garnet Heisler recalls that the boys did race "just for the fun of it, after all the Gloucester fellows had come all that way. We thought they should at least get to row."

The next summer, 1971, the whole country was riding a high. Prime Minister Pierre Elliot Trudeau was vacationing on a cross-country tour with his new bride, Margaret, and would be making a visit to the Fisheries Exhibition in Lunenburg. It was to be the first time in the thirty-five year history of the event that a sitting prime minister would visit. Sherman Zwicker was then mayor of the town of Lunenburg and remembers the excitement and the build up to the prime ministerial visit.

"We, of course, were all very excited at the prospect of having Mr. Trudeau come to Lunenburg, particularly during Exhibition. As you can imagine, we went to a great deal of trouble to make sure everything was just as it should be," says Zwicker. In the hours leading up to his arrival, there was some consternation that the visit might not come off as planned due to Yarmouth airport being fogged in. Sunny skies prevailed in the end and the Prime Minister and Mrs. Trudeau were welcomed to the town of Lunenburg and the unique Fisheries Exhibition.

Sherman Zwicker remembers the details with a laugh. "In those days, everyone put on their Sunday best for Exhibition. Even the spectators who lined the wharf on watersports day wore a shirt and tie, or a summer dress for the ladies. So everyone involved — all the town officials and Exhibition committee members — had of course dressed to a tee in their finest suits of clothes, buttoned up fit for royalty. And here comes our Prime Minister, the honoured guest — dressed appropriately for a seaside exhibition in jeans and a t-shirt with a pair of sandals on his feet. You had to laugh."

Prime Minister Trudeau was presented with a framed print of a doryman, symbolizing the traditions of the town and providing him with a souvenir of his day at the Exhibition. He watched as Gerald Mossman and Sonny Heisler were once again presented with the trophy for the senior international dory racing championship.

By 1972, there was a sense for some that things were starting to change at the Fisheries exhibition. While Lunenburg, in its small town east coast culture, was insulated to some degree from the social turmoil of the day, it was certain that the times, as they say were "a-changin'." And for Gerald Mossman, some of the fun had gone out of dory racing.

"We'd made a habit of winning. I guess for some of the spectators that was getting dull. I'd have people say to me, 'Well, I knew you were going to win anyway so I didn't bother coming to watch you.' There was a time when the wharves would just be packed with people for the dory races and that was starting to dwindle. For me, I guess it was just time to get on with my life. Put up my racing oars and move on to something new."

Sonny was once again without a partner, but not for long. He'd turn first to the fellow that he knew best, the fellow who still had something to prove — his brother Garnet.

With Hilary Dombrowski and Jack Sulton slated to race for the U.S., Sonny tempted Garnet with the idea of a race for revenge — a chance for the two of them to erase the stain on their record of their earlier loss to Dombrowski and Sulton. They would then go down in history as the victors, not the vanquished (as they had been in 1966).

It was Heisler and Heisler together again for the Canadian elimination races in the summer of 1972. Settling back into their old rhythm, the brothers took up their oars to face Jack and Hilary again — this time in Lunenburg waters. As much as Dombrowski and Sulton had wanted to defeat the invincible Heislers back in '66, the Heisler brothers wanted this race — their first together in six years — to be all theirs.

As luck would have it, Garnet went to the line that day with three cracked ribs, broken two days before the race while "racking around" with a fellow sixty pounds heavier than himself.

"I didn't tell Sonny until we were headed for the start line," says Garnet, " I told Sonny then I'd had an accident, I got a bad shot of ribs. If we get a jump on these guys, don't slack up. Keep going. If we get a jump, we gotta hold it. I couldn't believe that these are the guys that beat me before in a dory and here they were looking at me again. I kept telling Sonny, don't you slack off. Keep what we got. Don't give 'em nothin'."

And so it was that with Sonny pulling his heart out in the stern and Garnet stroking from the bow, indifferent to his cracked ribs, they turned the tables on history and took down the American pair.

"It was the race I enjoyed the best," Garnet recalls, "Sweet revenge. I wanted it badly. I knew in '66 if we had trained, things could have been different. This was our chance to prove it to ourselves, and to everyone else. Don't get me wrong — Jack and Hilary are the finest kind of guys. They've got a lot of class, they're damn good rowers, and they're great sportsmen. But, by God, I wanted to beat them."

Sonny and Garnet went on to win five more international trophies before Garnet called it quits for the final time, retiring after winning in Gloucester in 1975. Sherman Zwicker made a moving speech in front of the crowd gathered for the trophy presentations to honour Garnet's great career in one of the best dory racing partnerships ever.

"It was quite a night, I tell you," says Garnet, "my mother and father had both come to Gloucester to watch Sonny and I race together for the last time. It was one of only two times my mother made the trip to Gloucester. Then to have Sherman Zwicker, the mayor of Lunenburg, give a tribute to me — well, it was pretty powerful, I'll just say that."

For the remainder of the 1970s, Sonny would take international trophies five more times, winning with partners David Croft once, and Tim Atkinson four times. As the turbulent 1970s came to a close in '79, so did the era of total dominance by the Canadians, in general, and by the Heisler family, in particular. Sonny Heisler, and his partner Tim Atkinson (who traded Canadian elimination victories back and forth with oarsmen Walter Nickerson and Brian Cotter from Lockeport, Nova Scotia from 1976 through 1978) raced together for the last time in Gloucester on June 30th, 1979. Then, like his brother and father before him, Sonny, who had won thirty-two international races in a career that spanned a quarter century, put away his oars. The way was cleared for new heroes to take up the challenge — to row, with grit and determination and strength, to a place in the hearts of the people of New England and the Maritimes. To do what dorymen had done for centuries, pull together and against one another for the simple pleasure of seeing who could make a wooden boat glide fastest through the waves of the North Atlantic.

Chapter 6

The 1980s and into the 1990s

In spite of forecasts for the fishing industry that had newspaper reports as early as 1974 predicting decline, the 1980s were boom times for Lunenburg and Gloucester. However, the days of the traditional Grand Banks schooner fishery were long over, and the inshore fishery no longer supported the numbers that it once did. Traditional skills like dory rowing and trawl baiting were no longer relevant to the industry of the day.

The 1980s were the glory days of the offshore. Trawler fishermen and offshore scallop fishermen enjoyed record catches and high incomes working aboard hundred and sixty foot trawlers. Life as a fishermen then as now, was by no means a walk on easy street, but many tasks and skills demanded by the job were vastly different from those of the first years of the Exhibition. Trawler fishermen now competed in net mending contests — the natural evolution of the trawl baiting contests of the schooner days. And scallop fishermen competed not only to see who was the fastest scallop shucker, but also held competitions to challenge one another at ring linking — a job particular to offshore scallop dragging technology.

In the midst of change, the traditions established first by the International Fishermen's trophy series and then by the International Dory Racing series held firm. It might not now, in the midst of widespread and rapid technological change, have much meaning in the day to day lives of the participants, but to Gloucester and Lunenburg, dory racing mattered. Pride was at stake and that competitive spirit of the world's two most prominent fishery ports could only be fully satisfied by a competition that pitted one boat against another.

In the vacuum left by Sonny's retirement, a fierce rivalry at the oars developed. A new family of Canadian stars emerged, who would pitch themselves time and again against an equally powerful and successful team from the United States.

A look at the record book for the first half of this decade tells the tale. In the twelve international races held between 1981 and 1986, the trophy went to Canadians Avery Henneberry and Wesley Henneberry five times, and to Americans Tim Rose and Scott Morrisey five times. The two trophies not taken by these pairs were won by Scott Morrissey rowing with his brother Alan and by Marty Henneberry (younger brother of Avery and Wesley's) rowing with partner Jim Gray.

For the Henneberrys of Sambro, Nova Scotia, the rise to the limelight came as a result of family teamwork and a life lived on the water. "We grew up on the water," says Avery Henneberry, the oldest of the four brothers from the small community outside of Halifax. "We fish for a living, all four of us, doing just about any type of fishing you could think of. Some inshore, some offshore. With the four of us brothers working together — we have different boats, but we're all in it together — we could work out a way for some of us to be training and some of us to be working."

Avery, the oldest, was the first to start rowing competitively. "Gus Reyno and I would compete in some of the smaller races around here, in Sambro and Prospect. Nothing big like Lunenburg, just little community races, but we always won. So some of the elders of the community thought we should head down to Lunenburg to give that a try — it was the big one, you know. Lunenburg for a rower was the one that you wanted to win."

Avery and Gus rowed together once at Lunenburg in 1978. Still teenagers, Avery just seventeen and Gus nineteen, the pair won their elimination heat to take on the big guns in the Canadian finals. "We didn't win, I remember that," says Avery, "But we did all right." In fact, the two young men placed a close third to champions Heisler and Atkinson, and veterans Walter Nickerson and Brian Cotter from Lunenburg, finishing just twelve seconds behind the Nickerson/Cotter dory. For two young rowers in such

Avery (left) and Wesley (right) of the renowned rowing Henneberry family pose with Deborah Rattray at the presentation of the 1981 Senior Championship trophy.
Photo by Terry Conrad, Lunenburg, N.S.

vaunted company, it was an impressive performance and it left Avery Henneberry with a thirst for something more.

"Things worked out well when Wesley and I started to row together. We fished on the same boat so we would be in, ashore, at the same times and could train together." When Wesley and Avery began their rowing career together, they quickly established their place in the top ranks of the international competitions.

"We certainly had our fair share of close races," Avery says, "I have the highest respect for the Morrissey brothers, Scott and Alan from Gloucester, and Scott's partner Tim Rose. It was always a tough race between the two teams and the trophies went back and forth for all the years we raced against one another. I think it's safe to say both teams had a lot of respect for the other.

"After Sonny Heisler retired, and I just raced against him the

Greg Smith (left) and Marty Henneberry, pictured here with 1981 Queen of the Sea Belinda Ernst, were a powerful force in the Junior division.

Photo by Terry Conrad, Lunenburg,, N.S.

once, his last year, we were sort of the new generation, the Morrisseys and us Henneberrys. Ours were the new names in the newspapers in the 1980s and into the '90s. We'd go down to Lunenburg to race from Sambro and we made our mark there and in Gloucester."

The four Henneberrys — Avery, the oldest, then Wesley, followed by Marty and Clark, the youngest — raced more than a dozen times in various configurations, depending on who was ashore and who had time to train together. Marty and Clark enjoyed success as juniors, Marty rowing with partner Greg Smith and Clark taking up the oars with Douglas Cassibo (the only hearing impaired athlete to record international wins) and later with partner Paul Drew. Rowing with his youngest brother, Clark, Avery would go on to win the international trophy in 1992 and 1993.

In 1982, as the Henneberrys were in the early days of their

play for dory racing fame, the two rowers who had first taken up the international challenge for Canada were being recognized for their remarkable contribution to the sport of dory racing and to the social history of Nova Scotia.

One evening in April of 1982, Lloyd Heisler and Russell Langille got themselves dressed in their best suits, and snugged up their good ties around beneath their chins. Older, but unbent, they stepped proudly out with Lloyd's wife Jenny, and their good friends Sherman and Barbara Zwicker, to head for Halifax. Gathering with other members of the Heisler and Langille clans, they made their way to the gala dinner being held for the new slate of inductees into Nova Scotia's Sports Hall of Fame.

For twenty one years, Lloyd and Russell had rowed together, undefeated. They had brought home the first international trophy for their sport, bestowing a new glory on the fishermen of the province in the years following the reign of the *Bluenose*. Lloyd Heisler and Russell Langille were, as their profile in the publication *Beyond Heroes* states: ". . . remarkable, well–loved, hearty ambassadors of the hard–working people they represented. . . Langille and Heisler, like the boats they used, were not built for speed, but

Legendary rowing champions Russell Langille (left) and Lloyd Heisler at their induction into the Nova Scotia Sports Hall of Fame.

Courtesy of the Heisler Family

rather, were ideally suited to maintain a strong effort over a long period of time." And with their induction, they were duly honoured for that effort and their contribution.

Chapter 7

The Junior Competitors, the Women and the Over Forty Crowd

With the summer of 2002 marking the fiftieth anniversary of the international dory races, it must be noted that the popularity of the senior division — the only division to be hitting the fifty year mark — gave birth to three other divisions that were incorporated into the bi-annual international events.

For years, before the divisions for junior and female rowers became part of the duelling match races between Gloucester and Lunenburg, teenagers and women had been competing against each other in local events. In 1957 Lunenburg's exceptional female athletes Josephine O'Connor and Annabelle Best finished *one-two* in the ladies' swimming competition before climbing into a dory to beat Mary Demone and Helen Dodge for the ladies' dory race prize.

Regular races for female competitors in Lunenburg were difficult to establish. There were many more young women interested in vying for the crown and sash bestowed upon the *Queen of the Sea*, winner of the beauty contest, than those looking to prove themselves at the oars of a six hundred pound wooden boat. As social customs changed over the course of time, women's dory racing would come into its own. Indeed, in the later 1980s and 1990s, the women's division became hotly contested year after year.

In the women's division as in the others, family ties bred suc-

Canadian women Chrissy Atwood and Nicole Jones pull into the lead in a race against Angela Morrissey and Julie Geary.
Courtesy of The Lunenburg Fishermen's Picnic & Reunion

cess. Carolyn Brackett represented Canada in seven international competitions, winning the trophy twice with her partner Sherry Purcell, then going on to win the Canadian eliminations five times when her sister Shawna joined her in the dory. The Brackett women, rowing together, took the Gloucester trophy against Angela Morrissey and Valerie Marino in 1993.

In recent years, Canada's Chrissy Atwood and Nicole Jones have taken to the line against Angela Morrissey and Julie Geary of the United States in a rivalry mirroring that of the Henneberry and Morrissey match ups in the men's division, with the victories alternating almost from year to year.

It seems a fitting irony that as the women's dory racing division gathers growing strength, the venerable institution of the Exhibition's *Queen of the Sea* contest has all but disappeared.

In 1998, the newest division of the international races was created — the Over 40 Division for Men. It is a testament to the staying power of dory racing that this category was established. Oarsmen who are no longer competitive in the intense battles for the seniors' trophies, but are still keen to compete, test themselves against their peers, contesting against one another for the bragging rights of another international victory. In the years following its inception, a powerful team from Lunenburg dominated this division: Dale Cook and David Croft. The first five international trophies awarded for Men Over 40 were presented to the team of Cook and Croft. David Croft, who had been a junior during the "bucket scandal of 1970" was back at the oars and winning once again.

Familiar names from the senior and junior champions record books are appearing each year in the race for the "Over 40" trophy. Names like David Swim.

In 1967 seventeen year old David Swim, from Clark's Harbour, rowing with his fifteen year old brother Larry beat out four other teams to represent Canada in the International Junior race in Lunenburg. The Swim brothers pulled off a stunning upset against American juniors Kenneth Morris and Ed Parnell, three time champions rowing for their last time as juniors. Parnell and Morris had beaten David Swim and his partner Steven Nickerson two match-ups in a row before David turned to his brother for partnership, as many a successful oarsman had done before him.

In a year when the Canadian seniors yawned all the way to the finish line with a lead of more than ten dory lengths, it was the juniors who gave the crowd a thrill.

Behind slightly at the gun, the Swim brothers executed the classic Canadian manoeuver neatly nipping around the buoy, picking up almost a full dory length. They held their lead as both teams pulled hard to the finish, pacing themselves off the American rowers, speeding up whenever a challenge came. At the wire, the youngsters from Clark's Harbour had two dory lengths on the veterans Parnell and Morris, and they had the crowd roaring with delight. Swim and Swim went on to take two more international trophies.

In 2000, Ed Parnell and David Swim rowed out to the start line to challenge each other once again. Parnell paired this time with John Morris and Swim with rower David Nickerson. The Americans got the jump on the Canadian oarsmen and, thirty three years after the fact, Ed Parnell snatched victory back from the upstart Swim. You can't help but wonder if his victory was that much sweeter for the wait!

While there has never been a junior winning streak with quite the same resonance that the Canadians enjoyed in the seniors, the junior oarsmen have long been crowd-pleasers. Occasionally, the junior race was won by a huge margin to the delight of the home town crowd (as it was in 1977). In that year juniors Ian Creaser (whose father David with his partner Cyril Ernst had broken the Heisler- Langille course record in 1960) and Keith Levy took to the line against the American team of Sam Scola and Vito Giacalone. "It was blowing hard that day," Ian Creaser recalls, "and if there's one thing Lunenburg rowers know how to do, it's row in the wind. The Americans never quite got the hang of that the way the Canadians did. So that day when it was blowing, Keith and I rowed a good strong race, but Sam and Vito were all over the course. I think they were just about under the wharf at one point." And Creaser and Levy won that day by an astounding two minute margin, almost unheard of in the latter days of dory racing.

Other times, the battle for the junior trophy was so intense, so closely fought, that only a hair's breadth separated the two teams, giving the crowd a spine-tingling photo finish. In 1999 Canadian juniors Barrett Risser and Ryan Conrad faced down an American team with a family history of success at the oars — young Zach Morrissey and John Sulton Jr. — in a race that showed the true grit of dorymen from both the United States and Canada. The race was ultimately won by what was estimated to be in the hundredths of a second, with Risser and Conrad snatching the win. Like many a rower before them, the boys had put their heart and soul, and every last ounce of their strength into winning, and both had to be helped from the wharf as they were having trouble walking after the dramatic finish.

With the junior international races well-established in 1958, there have been many champions that began their rowing careers as young men and went on to great success in the senior ranks. Bridgewater, Nova Scotia's Tim Atkinson took three international trophies consecutively as a junior before joining the senior ranks and partnering with Sonny Heisler for four impressive senior victories in the late 1970s. And throughout the forty-four years of junior competition, the family dynasties that ruled the sport are clearly evident. Names like Heisler, Eisnor, Morrissey, and Henneberry appear in the lists of junior champions time and again. Brothers, cousins, sons and even daughters picking up the sport and carrying on the family's winning ways like their fathers, grand-

The 1999 Junior Champions Barrett Risser (foreground) and Ryan Conrad grabbed victory in a photo finish.
Photo by Susan Corkum-Greek, Lighthouse Publishing Ltd.,
Bridgewater, N.S.

fathers and uncles before them.

Two more brother combinations brought junior trophies home ten times in the mid 1980s and early 1990s. Dennis and Grant Garrison grabbed four international victories while rowing junior for Canada, followed by a stunning six wins in a row by brothers Aaron and Terry Miller.

Throughout the years, the junior oarsmen of the international dory races enjoyed not only the sportsmanship and athleticism of the challenge, but winning the elimination races in their division races has also provided many a young man with an opportunity to travel that might not have otherwise been forthcoming.

Michael Spindler, a junior rower from Lunenburg, had listened to the stories of the fun of the Gloucester St. Peter's Fiesta from his sister Kris Ann, a rower who twice competed for Canada at the Gloucester event.

"My mum and dad had both gone with Kris Ann to Gloucester, and I had to stay home," Michael says. "It sounded like so much fun, they all had such a great time, I wished that I could have gone too. When I told Dad I wanted to go to Gloucester

The 1989 Canadian contingent returning from Gloucester. Pictured here, from left are Toddy Dempsey, Edwin Dempsey, Grant Garrison and Dennis Garrison, Edward Dempsey, W.J. Parsons of the Canadian Coast Guard, Gerald MacKinnon and Junior Boudreau.

Staff photo, Lighthouse Publishing Ltd., Bridgewater, N.S.

sometime, he told me the only way I was going to get there was if I rowed myself there. So I did."

Michael and his partner Chris Jordan practised three times a week, rowing for at least an hour each time out and training on the Lunenburg Harbour course. They earned the right to go to Gloucester in an uncontested row in 1999 at the Canadian eliminations, to finish a painful twelve seconds behind Americans Zach Morrissey and John Sulton, Jr. in Gloucester. Undaunted, Jordan and Spindler returned to take the Canadian eliminations again and row in Lunenburg against the experienced American juniors. Michael Spindler, at fifteen, waits for his father to put the dory in the water in spring, ready to spend his evenings on the water with his friend Chris, pulling their way towards dreams of an international win.

Chapter 8

The Tradition Continues

The fishing industry is in a state that would have been inconceivable to the men who once plied the rich grounds of the Grand Banks with dories stacked on decks beneath the tight canvas sails of their schooners. A new millennium has begun, and for towns like Lunenburg, it has been a time to rethink their place in the world. Tourism has taken a place of equal importance to that of the fishery in a town that calls itself "The Fishing Capital of Canada." The Fisheries Exhibition has downsized and relocated to a new and more appropriate location on the waterfront wharves. But in the face of all this change, steadfast traditions stand tall.

The "Yanks" and the "Novies" still take one another on in brightly coloured wooden boats cresting the waters of Lunenburg Harbour. Pride still matters. Strength and skill with a pair of oars are still admired. And after the rowing is over, friends from both sides of the border still get together for a drink and a yarn in a waterfront bar.

Lloyd and Russell had taught Nova Scotian dorymen much. Not only by their example, but through the time they spent coaching young rowers — Russell beginning with young Garnet and his cousin Lawrence Ernst. If there was anything Canadian rowers learned from Heisler and Langille's legacy it was that the turn mattered.

The Americans often brought impressive power to the game, strong rowers with ample weight to manhandle the six hundred pound dories, but it was the Canadian finesse for an agile turn around the buoys that often made the winning difference.

In one newspaper report after another throughout the fifty

Roger Atwood (stern) and Gary Sears represented Canada in the 2000 and 2001 Senior Division.
Photo by Jodie Turner, Lighthouse Publishing Ltd., Bridgewater, N.S.

year history of the race, mention was made year after year of the Canadians gaining their lead at the turn.

"It ain't about power," Lloyd once said to a young rower in Gloucester, "You gotta know how to handle a dory. You gotta learn how to make her do what you want. Keep working at it, it'll come."

In the summer of 2001, on an August day in Lunenburg, the undefeated team of Todd Dempsey (whose family has put many a great rower on the line for Canada over the past fifty years) and Danny Brackett (himself from a family of oarsmen and women) were the latest in a long line of Canadian oarsman to use the buoy as the make or break point in their race as they took to the line against the Americans in a good breeze.

Like Russell Langille (who could unerringly guide a dory straight to the mark, as if he were drawn there by a magnet) and Sonny Heisler (whose skill with the oars could turn a dory on a dime) Brackett and Dempsey knew their chance to defend their title lay in their refined skills as much as their muscle.

When the Canadians positioned themselves unusually high

on the line, well up from the buoy, the Americans thought they had the race in the bag. With a good lead on the first leg to the turn, the Gloucester rowers were confident, until they realized that the wind had pushed them off their chosen course, and they struggled to gain position before the buoy. Brackett and Dempsey, on the other hand, let the wind do the work for them, gliding gently into position as they pulled. With fluid grace, they took the Americans on the turn and headed for home in the lead.

It would have made Lloyd and Russell proud. And they would have undoubtedly called for a drink to toast yet another successful race by a pair of undefeated Canadians.

Sonny Heisler, thirty-two time international champion, shown here embracing competitor Woody Greek in a bear hug while their dorymates, Gerald Mossman and Gerald Greely look on.

Courtesy of Knickle's Studio and Gallery, Lunenburg, N.S.

Appendix of Champions

This appendix is the result of months of research as a single source of accurate results has not been kept throughout the fifty year history of the races. In the case of discrepancies between American records and Canadian records, the home nation's results were considered the more accurate — therefore, for American rowers, American records were referenced, for Canadian rowers, Canadian sources were referenced.

Winners	Senior Men		Runners-up
Lloyd Heisler Russell Langille	Gloucester	1952	Steven D'Amico Jerry Nicastro
Lloyd Heisler Russell Langille	Lunenburg	1952	"Bunt" Davis Fred Purdy
Lloyd Heisler Russell Langille	Gloucester	1953	Gordon MacLane Gerry Holmes
Dick Nagle Gerald Dempsey	Lunenburg	1953	Edward Josephson Fred Purdy
Lloyd Heisler Russell Langille	Gloucester	1954	"Bunt" Davis William Merchant
Lloyd Heisler Russell Langille	Lunenburg	1954	"Bunt" Davis William Merchant
Lloyd Heisler Russell Langille	Gloucester	1955	Warren McGregor James Carter
Lloyd Heisler Russell Langille	Lunenburg	1955	Warren McGregor James Carter
Gerald Schwartz Gerry Hannams	Gloucester	1956	Warren McGregor James Carter
Gerald Schwartz Gerry Hannams	Lunenburg	1956	Warren McGregor James Carter
Gerald Schwartz Gerry Hannams	Gloucester	1957	Arthur Moon James Carter
Dick Nagle Gerald Dempsey	Lunenburg	1957	Arthur Moon James Carter
Robert Harrington Charles Moon	Gloucester	1958	Dick Nagle Gerald Dempsey
Dick Nagle Gerald Dempsey	Lunenburg	1958	Robert Harrington Charles Moon
Robert Harrington Charles Moon	Gloucester	1959	David Creaser Cyril Ernst
David Creaser Cyril Ernst	Lunenburg	1959	Robert Harrington Charles Moon
David Creaser Cyril Ernst	Gloucester	1960	Joseph Kelly Dick Justice
Sonny Heisler Leonard Eisnor	Lunenburg	1960	Joseph Kelly Dick Justice
Sonny Heisler Leonard Eisnor	Gloucester	1961	Richard Hastings Harold Read
Sonny Heisler Leonard Eisnor	Lunenburg	1961	George Hastings Harold Read

🇨🇦	Sonny Heisler Leonard Eisnor	Gloucester	1962	Robert Rose George Hastings
🇨🇦	Sonny Heisler Leonard Eisnor	Lunenburg	1962	Robert Rose George Hastings
🇨🇦	Sonny Heisler Leonard Eisnor	Gloucester	1963	Joseph Carpenter Arthur Moon
🇨🇦	Sonny Heisler Garnet Heisler	Lunenburg	1963	Joseph Carpenter Arthur Moon
🇨🇦	Sonny Heisler Garnet Heisler	Gloucester	1964	Michael Dearborn Frank Lord
🇨🇦	Sonny Heisler Garnet Heisler	Lunenburg	1964	Michael Dearborn Frank Lord
🇨🇦	Sonny Heisler Garnet Heisler	Gloucester	1965	Robert Greeke Philip Hoysradt
🇨🇦	Sonny Heisler Garnet Heisler	Lunenburg	1965	Robert Greeke Philip Hoysradt
🇺🇸	Hilary Dombrowski John Sulton	Gloucester	1966	Sonny Heisler Garnet Heisler
🇨🇦	Sonny Heisler Gerald Mossman	Lunenburg	1966	Hilary Dombrowski John Sulton
🇨🇦	Sonny Heisler Gerald Mossman	Gloucester	1967	Robert Greeke John Sulton
🇨🇦	Sonny Heisler Gerald Mossman	Lunenburg	1967	Robert Greeke John Sulton
🇨🇦	Sonny Heisler Gerald Mossman	Gloucester	1968	Hilary Dombrowski John Sulton
🇨🇦	Sonny Heisler Gerald Mossman	Lunenburg	1968	Hilary Dombrowski John Sulton
🇨🇦	Sonny Heisler Gerald Mossman	Gloucester	1969	Bill Lord John Messenger
🇨🇦	Sonny Heisler Gerald Mossman	Lunenburg	1969	Bill Lord John Messenger
🇨🇦	Sonny Heisler Gerald Mossman	Gloucester	1970	Robert Greeke Gerald Greely
🇨🇦	Sonny Heisler Gerald Mossman	Lunenburg	1970	Robert Greeke Gerald Greely
🇨🇦	Sonny Heisler Gerald Mossman	Gloucester	1971	Robert Greeke Gerald Greely
🇨🇦	Sonny Heisler Gerald Mossman	Lunenburg	1971	Robert Greeke Gerald Greely

🇨🇦 Sonny Heisler Gerald Mossman	Gloucester	1972	Hilary Dombrowski John Sulton
🇨🇦 Sonny Heisler Garnet Heisler	Lunenburg	1972	Hilary Dombrowski John Sulton
🇨🇦 Sonny Heisler Garnet Heisler	Gloucester	1973	Paul Mondello Richard Medico
🇨🇦 Sonny Heisler Garnet Heisler	Lunenburg	1973	Paul Mondello Richard Medico
🇨🇦 Sonny Heisler Garnet Heisler	Gloucester	1974	Mike Cody John Sulton
🇨🇦 Sonny Heisler Garnet Heisler	Lunenburg	1974	Mike Cody John Sulton
🇨🇦 Sonny Heisler Garnet Heisler	Gloucester	1975	Paul Mondello Richard Medico
🇨🇦 Sonny Heisler David Croft	Lunenburg	1975	Paul Mondello Richard Medico
🇺🇸 John Morris Gary Morris	Gloucester	1976	Sonny Heisler David Croft
🇨🇦 Sonny Heisler Tim Atkinson	Lunenburg	1976	John Sulton Ed Parnell
🇨🇦 Sonny Heisler Tim Atkinson	Gloucester	1977	Steve Goodick Steve Moore
🇨🇦 Walter Nickerson Brian Cotter	Lunenburg	1977	Steve Goodick Steve Moore
🇨🇦 Walter Nickerson Brian Cotter	Gloucester	1978	Steve Goodick Steve Moore
🇨🇦 Sonny Heisler Tim Atkinson	Lunenburg	1978	Steve Goodick Steve Moore
🇨🇦 Sonny Heisler Tim Atkinson	Gloucester	1979	Winn Story John Montgomery
🇨🇦 Walter Nickerson Brian Cotter	Lunenburg	1979	Steve Goodick Steve Moore
🇨🇦 Walter Nickerson Brian Cotter	Gloucester	1980	Scott Morrissey Jay Prince
🇨🇦 Walter Nickerson Brian Cotter	Lunenburg	1980	John Morris Gary Morris
🇺🇸 Tim Rose Scott Morrissey	Gloucester	1981	Linden Tanner Bobby Crinion
🇨🇦 Avery Henneberry Wesley Henneberry	Lunenburg	1981	John Morris Gary Morris

🇨🇦	Avery Henneberry Wesley Henneberry	Gloucester	1982	Tim Rose Scott Morrissey
🇨🇦	Avery Henneberry Wesley Henneberry	Lunenburg	1982	Tim Rose Scott Morrissey
🇺🇸	Tim Rose Scott Morrissey	Gloucester	1983	Avery Henneberry Wesley Henneberry
🇺🇸	Tim Rose Scott Morrissey	Lunenburg	1983	Mike Currie Kenneth MacDonald
🇺🇸	Tim Rose Scott Morrissey	Gloucester	1984	Mike Currie Kenneth MacDonald
🇨🇦	Avery Henneberry Wesley Henneberry	Lunenburg	1984	Tim Rose Scott Morrissey
🇺🇸	Tim Rose Scott Morrissey	Gloucester	1985	Marty Henneberry Jim Gray
🇺🇸	Scott Morrissey Alan Morrissey	Lunenburg	1985	Avery Henneberry Wesley Henneberry
🇨🇦	Marty Henneberry Jim Gray	Gloucester	1986	Mike Frontiera Jay Giacalone
🇨🇦	Avery Henneberry Wesley Henneberry	Lunenburg	1986	Scott Morrissey Alan Morrissey
🇨🇦	Brent Dempsey Craig Dempsey	Gloucester	1987	Scott Morrissey Alan Morrissey
🇨🇦	Todd Dempsey Danny Brackett	Lunenburg	1987	Scott Morrissey Alan Morrissey
🇨🇦	Todd Dempsey Danny Brackett	Gloucester	1988	Tony Frontiero Steve Goodick
🇺🇸	Scott Morrissey Alan Morrissey	Lunenburg	1988	Brent Dempsey Craig Dempsey
🇺🇸	Scott Morrissey Alan Morrissey	Gloucester	1989	Todd Cranston Edward Dempsey
🇨🇦	Todd Dempsey Brent Dempsey	Lunenburg	1989	Tony Frontiero Joe Cominelli
🇨🇦	Todd Dempsey Brent Dempsey	Gloucester	1990	Tony Frontiero Joe Cominelli
🇨🇦	Todd Dempsey Brent Dempsey	Lunenburg	1990	Tony Frontiero Joe Cominelli
🇺🇸	Tony Frontiero Joe Cominelli	Gloucester	1991	Todd Cranston Edward Dempsey
🇺🇸	Tony Frontiero Joe Cominelli	Lunenburg	1991	Todd Dempsey Brent Dempsey

🇺🇸	Scott Morrissey Mike Morrissey	Gloucester	1992	Todd Dempsey Brent Dempsey	
🇨🇦	Clark Henneberry Avery Henneberry	Lunenburg	1992	Scott Morrissey Mike Morrissey	
🇺🇸	Scott Morrissey Mike Morrissey	Gloucester	1993	Todd Dempsey Todd Cranston	
🇨🇦	Clark Henneberry Avery Henneberry	Lunenburg	1993	Joe Cominelli Alan Morrissey	
🇺🇸	Joe Cominelli Alan Morrissey	Gloucester	1994	Trevor Lohnes Brent Knickle	
🇺🇸	Joe Cominelli Alan Morrissey	Lunenburg	1994	Clark Henneberry Avery Henneberry	
🇺🇸	Joe Cominelli Mike Morrissey	Gloucester	1995	Ed Dempsey Charles Clow	
🇨🇦	Todd Dempsey Danny Brackett	Lunenburg	1995	Joe Cominelli Mike Morrissey	
🇺🇸	Joe Cominelli Mike Morrissey	Gloucester	1996	David Croft Jr. Trevor Kidson	
🇺🇸	Joe Cominelli Mike Morrissey	Lunenburg	1996	David Croft Jr. Trevor Kidson	
🇺🇸	Mike Morrissey Scott Morrissey	Gloucester	1997	Wayne Jensen Trevor Lohnes	
🇺🇸	Mike Morrissey Scott Morrissey	Lunenburg	1997	Arron Miller Terry Miller	
🇺🇸	Joe Cominelli Mike Morrissey	Gloucester	1998	Richard Heisler Richard Tanner	
🇨🇦	Todd Dempsey Danny Brackett	Lunenburg	1998	Joe Cominelli Mike Morrissey	
🇨🇦	Todd Dempsey Danny Brackett	Gloucester	1999	Alan Morrissey Scott Morrissey	
🇺🇸	Alan Morrissey Scott Morrissey	Lunenburg	1999	Brent Dempsey Roy Dempsey	
🇺🇸	Joe Cominelli Scott Morrissey	Gloucester	2000	George Atwood Anthony Nickerson	
🇺🇸	Joe Cominelli Scott Morrissey	Lunenburg	2000	Roger Atwood Gary Sears	
🇺🇸	John Morris Ed Parnell	Gloucester	2001	Roger Atwood Gary Sears	
🇨🇦	Todd Dempsey Danny Brackett	Lunenburg	2001	Alan Morrissey Joe Cominelli	

	Winners	Junior Men		Runners-up
🇨🇦	Gordon Eisnor Leonard Eisnor	Lunenburg	1957	No U.S. Team
🇺🇸	Carlton Eckborg George Hastings	Gloucester	1958	Peter Pelham Michael Pelham
🇨🇦	Gordon Eisnor Leonard Eisnor	Lunenburg	1958	Carlton Eckborg George Hastings
🇨🇦	Gordon Eisnor Leonard Eisnor	Gloucester	1959	Carlton Eckborg George Hastings
🇨🇦	Gordon Eisnor Leonard Eisnor	Lunenburg	1959	Carlton Eckborg George Hastings
🇨🇦	Gordon Eisnor Leonard Eisnor	Gloucester	1960	Richard Hasnoot Richard Fressenden
🇨🇦	Garnet Heisler Lawrence Ernst	Lunenburg	1960	Richard Hasnoot Richard Fressenden
🇨🇦	Garnet Heisler Lawrence Ernst	Gloucester	1961	Richard Hasnoot Charles Bateman
🇨🇦	Garnet Heisler Lawrence Ernst	Lunenburg	1961	Charles Bateman Richard Hasnoot
🇨🇦	Garnet Heisler Lawrence Ernst	Gloucester	1962	Charles Bateman Richard Hasnoot
🇨🇦	Garnet Heisler Lawrence Ernst	Lunenburg	1962	Charles Bateman Richard Hasnoot
🇨🇦	Garnet Heisler Lawrence Ernst	Gloucester	1963	Ronald Ottens Robert Greeke
🇺🇸	Ronald Ottens Robert Greeke	Lunenburg	1963	Sidney Spencer Fred Scott
🇺🇸	Hilary Dombrowski Philip Hoysradt	Gloucester	1964	Sidney Spencer Fred Scott
🇺🇸	Hilary Dombrowski Philip Hoysradt	Lunenburg	1964	Linden Tanner Jim Kaulback
🇺🇸	Hilary Dombrowski Ronald Woodard	Gloucester	1965	Linden Tanner Jim Kaulback
🇺🇸	Hilary Dombrowski Ronald Woodard	Lunenburg	1965	Charles Ernst Linden Tanner
🇺🇸	Ken Morris Ed Parnell	Gloucester	1966	Charles Ernst Linden Tanner
🇺🇸	Ken Morris Ed Parnell	Lunenburg	1966	David Swim Stephen Nickerson
🇺🇸	Ken Morris Ed Parnell	Gloucester	1967	David Swim Stephen Nickerson
🇨🇦	David Swim Larry Swim	Lunenburg	1967	Ken Morris Ed Parnell

🇨🇦	David Swim Larry Swim	Gloucester	1968	Richard Greeke Paul Mondello
🇨🇦	David Swim Larry Swim	Lunenburg	1968	Richard Greeke Paul Mondello
🇺🇸	Gino Mondello Richard Greeke	Gloucester	1969	Gary Fox Richard Hannams
🇨🇦	Reid Risser David Croft	Lunenburg	1969	Gino Mondello Richard Greeke
🇨🇦	Reid Risser David Croft	Gloucester	1970	Steve Swett Richard Greeke
	No official Race (Steve Swett/Richard Greeke————	*Lunenburg*	*1970*	*No official Race* —Tim Atkinson/George Taylor)
🇨🇦	Tim Atkinson George Taylor	Gloucester	1971	Jeff Williams Leo Sharamitaro
🇨🇦	Tim Atkinson George Taylor	Lunenburg	1971	Jeff Williams Leo Sharamitaro
🇨🇦	Tim Atkinson George Taylor	Gloucester	1972	Leo Sharamitaro John Peterson
🇺🇸	Leo Sharamitaro John Peterson	Lunenburg	1972	Lloyd Tanner Scott Tanner
🇺🇸	John Dewolfe Terry Knuuttunen	Gloucester	1973	Lloyd Tanner Scott Tanner
🇺🇸	John Dewolfe Terry Knuuttunen	Lunenburg	1973	Lloyd Tanner Chris Tanner
🇨🇦	Lloyd Tanner Chris Tanner	Gloucester	1974	Tom Aiello John Mioni
🇨🇦	Charles Daurie Harold Forward	Lunenburg	1974	Tom Aiello John Mioni
🇺🇸	Winn Story John Montgomery	Gloucester	1975	Terry Skinner Stephen Russell
🇺🇸	Winn Story John Montgomery	Lunenburg	1975	Larry Tanner Jerome Romkey
🇺🇸	Winn Story John Montgomery	Gloucester	1976	Larry Tanner Jerome Romkey
🇺🇸	Winn Story John Montgomery	Lunenburg	1976	Todd Labrador John Jeremy
🇺🇸	Scott Morrissey Mike Morrissey	Gloucester	1977	Ian Creaser Keith Levy
🇨🇦	Ian Creaser Keith Levy	Lunenburg	1977	Sam Scola Vito Giacalone

Flag	Skippers	Port	Year	Opponents
🇨🇦	Ian Creaser Keith Levy	Gloucester	1978	Scott Morrissey Tim Rose
🇺🇸	Vito Giacalone Edward Hinckley	Lunenburg	1978	Danny Moody Tim Rhyno
🇺🇸	Vito Giacalone Edward Hinckley	Gloucester	1979	Danny Moody Tim Rhyno
🇺🇸	Vito Giacalone Edward Hinckley	Lunenburg	1979	Danny Moody Tim Rhyno
🇺🇸	Steve Davis Mark Favaloro	Gloucester	1980	Marty Henneberry Greg Smith
🇨🇦	Marty Henneberry Greg Smith	Lunenburg	1980	Steve Davis Mark Favaloro
🇨🇦	Marty Henneberry Greg Smith	Gloucester	1981	Steve Aiello Nick Sanfileppo
🇨🇦	Marty Henneberry Greg Smith	Lunenburg	1981	Mike Frontiera Tim Kennedy
🇺🇸	Joe Sanfileppo Mark Aiello	Gloucester	1982	Chris Power Bill Seymour
🇺🇸	Jay Giacalone Mike Frontiera	Lunenburg	1982	Amos Henneberry Robin Henneberry
🇺🇸	Jay Giacalone Mike Frontiera	Gloucester	1983	Amos Henneberry Robin Henneberry
🇺🇸	Jay Giacalone Mike Frontiera	Lunenburg	1983	Clark Henneberry Douglas Cassibo
🇨🇦	Clark Henneberry Douglas Cassibo	Gloucester	1984	Jay Giacalone Mike Frontiera
🇺🇸	Joe Sanfileppo Joe Favazzo	Lunenburg	1984	Clark Henneberry Paul Drew
🇺🇸	Joe Sanfileppo Joe Favazzo	Gloucester	1985	Clark Henneberry Paul Drew
🇨🇦	Clark Henneberry Paul Drew	Lunenburg	1985	Joe Sanfileppo Frank Sanfileppo
🇨🇦	Clark Henneberry Paul Drew	Gloucester	1986	Billy Edmonds Jerry Ciaramitaro
🇨🇦	Clark Henneberry Paul Drew	Lunenburg	1986	Billy Edmonds Jerry Ciaramitaro
🇺🇸	Jerry Ryan Frank Sanfileppo	Gloucester	1987	Robert Gosbee Kevin Clorey
🇨🇦	Dennis Garrison Grant Garrison	Lunenburg	1987	Scott Rowe Gus Sanfileppo
🇨🇦	Tony Allen Dean Schmiesser	Gloucester	1988	Kevin MacFarland Scott Rowe

🇨🇦	Dennis Garrison Grant Garrison	Lunenburg	1988	Scott Rowe Glenn Wheeler	
🇨🇦	Dennis Garrison Grant Garrison	Gloucester	1989	Scott Rowe Glenn Wheeler	
🇨🇦	Dennis Garrison Grant Garrison	Lunenburg	1989	Scott Rowe Glenn Wheeler	
🇨🇦	Aaron Miller Terry Miller	Gloucester	1990	Jude Lafavour Kevin MacFarland	
🇨🇦	Aaron Miller Terry Miller	Lunenburg	1990	Scott Cranston James Smith	
🇨🇦	Terry Miller LAaron Miller	Gloucester	1991	Geoff Thomas orenzo Billante	
🇨🇦	Terry Miller Aaron Miller	Lunenburg	1991	Geoff Thomas Kevin MacFarland	
🇨🇦	Terry Miller Aaron Miller	Gloucester	1992	Jeff Thomas Chad Johnson	
🇨🇦	Terry Miller Aaron Miller	Lunenburg	1992	Nick Novello Jerimiah Nicastro	
🇺🇸	Nick Novello Jerimiah Nicastro	Gloucester	1993	Aaron Miller Charles McGeoghean	
🇨🇦	Richard Tanner Terry Conrad	Lunenburg	1993	Nick Novello Jerimiah Nicastro	
🇺🇸	Chris Carvelas Jerry Cioliono	Gloucester	1994	Richard Tanner Terry Conrad	
🇨🇦	Mark Hunt Matthew Lambert	Lunenburg	1994	Jerry Cioliono Chris Karvelas	
🇨🇦	Mark Hunt Matthew Lambert	Gloucester	1995	Jay Novello Mike Novello	
🇺🇸	Danny Paone Robbie Benjamin	Lunenburg	1995	Mark Hunt Matthew Lambert	
🇺🇸	Danny Paone Robbie Benjamin	Gloucester	1996	Richard Tanner Richard Heisler	
🇨🇦	Matthew Ernst John Heisler	Lunenburg	1996	Mike Novello Pete Noble	
🇨🇦	Matthew Ernst John Heisler	Gloucester	1997	Zach Morrissey John Sulton Jr	
🇨🇦	Matthew Ernst John Heisler	Lunenburg	1997	Zach Morrissey John Sulton Jr	
🇺🇸	Zach Morrissey John Sulton Jr	Gloucester	1998	Matthew Ernst John Heisler	
🇺🇸	Zach Morrissey John Sulton Jr	Lunenburg	1998	Barrett Risser Chad Johnson	

🇨🇦	Barrett Risser Ryan Conrad	Gloucester	1999	Zach Morrissey John Sulton Jr
🇨🇦	Barrett Risser Ryan Conrad	Lunenburg	1999	Zach Morrissey John Sulton Jr
🇨🇦	Barrett Risser Ryan Conrad	Gloucester	2000	Vito Giacalone Chris Giacalone
🇺🇸	Zach Morrissey John Sulton Jr	Lunenburg	2000	Michael Spindler Chris Jordan
🇺🇸	Vito Giacalone Chris Giacalone	Gloucester	2001	Michael Spindler Chris Jordan
🇺🇸	Zach Morrissey John Sulton Jr	Lunenburg	2001	Michael Spindler Chris Jordan

	Winners	Women's		Runners-up
🇨🇦	Sherry Purcell Carolyn Brackett	Gloucester	1988	Gina Lampassi Laura Fleming
🇨🇦	Sherry Purcell Carolyn Brackett	Gloucester	1989	Doreen Scola Joanne Frontiero
🇺🇸	Gina Lampassi Laura Fleming	Lunenburg	1989	Unknown
🇺🇸	Gina Lampassi Laura Fleming	Gloucester	1990	No crew
🇨🇦	Unknown	Lunenburg	1990	Gina Lampassi Laura Fleming
🇺🇸	Gina Lampassi Laura Fleming	Gloucester	1991	Carolyn Brackett Shawna Brackett
🇺🇸	Gina Lampassi Laura Fleming	Lunenburg	1991	Carolyn Brackett Shawna Brackett
🇺🇸	Tammy Cominelli Gina Lampassi	Gloucester	1992	Carolyn Brackett Shawna Brackett
🇺🇸	Tammy Cominelli Gina Lampassi	Lunenburg	1992	Carolyn Brackett Shawna Brackett
🇨🇦	Carolyn Brackett Shawna Brackett	Gloucester	1993	Angela Morrissey Valerie Marino
🇺🇸	Tammy Cominelli Gina Lampassi	Lunenburg	1993	Janet March Michelle Risser
🇺🇸	Tammy Cominelli Gina Lampassi	Gloucester	1994	Janet March Michelle Risser
🇺🇸	Tammy Cominelli Gina Lampassi	Lunenburg	1994	Ann Marie Scott Melvina Hunt
🇺🇸	Tammy Cominelli Gina Lampassi	Gloucester	1995	Ann Marie Scott Melvina Hunt
🇺🇸	Tammy Cominelli Gina Lampassi	Lunenburg	1995	Ann Marie Scott Melvina Hunt
🇺🇸	Doreen Scola Angela Morrissey	Gloucester	1996	Kris Ann Spindler Kelly George
🇺🇸	Doreen Scola Angela Morrissey	Lunenburg	1996	Kris Ann Spindler Kelly George
🇺🇸	Doreen Scola Liza Warren	Gloucester	1997	Kris Ann Spindler Kelly George
🇺🇸	Doreen Scola Liza Warren	Lunenburg	1997	Lisa Tanner Jennifer Mills
🇺🇸	Tammy Cominelli Gina Lampassi	Gloucester	1998	Barbara Heisler Lisa Tanner
🇺🇸	Tammy Cominelli Gina Lampassi	Lunenburg	1998	Barbara Heisler Shannon McLeod

Appendix

🇺🇸	Julie Geary Angela Morrissey	Gloucester	1999	Barbara Heisler Shannon McLeod
🇨🇦	Chrissy Atwood Nicole Jones	Lunenburg	1999	Julie Geary Angela Morrissey
🇨🇦	Chrissy Atwood Nicole Jones	Gloucester	2000	Julie Gary Angela Morrissey
🇨🇦	Chrissy Atwood Nicole Jones	Lunenburg	2000	Joanne Frontiero Elin Afklinteberg
🇺🇸	Julie Geary Angela Morrissey	Gloucester	2001	Suzie Deraspe Carol Turbide
🇨🇦	Nicole Jones Natalie Symonds	Lunenburg	2001	Joanne Frontiero Elin Afklinteberg

69

	Winners	Over – 40		Runners-up
🇨🇦	Dale Cook David Croft	Gloucester	1996	Leonord Beiondo Anthony Militello
🇨🇦	Dale Cook David Croft	Lunenburg	1996	John Lefavour Anthony Militello
🇨🇦	Dale Cook David Croft	Gloucester	1997	Jack Alexander Tom Perkins
🇨🇦	Dale Cook David Croft	Lunenburg	1997	Leonord Beiondo Anthony Militello
🇨🇦	Dale Cook David Croft	Gloucester	1998	Jack Alexander Tom Perkins
🇨🇦	Garth Bell Roger Atwood	Lunenburg	1998	Jack Alexander John Lefavour
🇺🇸	John Morris Ed Parnell	Gloucester	1999	Roger Atwood Donnie Mahaney
🇨🇦	Roger Atwood Gary Sears	Lunenburg	1999	John Morris Ed Parnell
🇨🇦	Roger Atwood Gary Sears	Gloucester	2000	Bernie Cranston Jack Alexander
🇺🇸	John Morris Ed Parnell	Lunenburg	2000	David Swim David Nickerson
🇨🇦	David Swim David Nickerson	Gloucester	2001	Joe Balbo Sam Scola
🇨🇦	Davis Atwood Mark Symonds	Lunenburg	2001	Bernie Cranston Dana Josephson